ENERGY
TECHNOLOGY

by Kathryn Hulick

Content Consultant

Sunil S. Mehendale

Assistant Professor, School of Technology

Michigan Technological University

Essential Library

An Imprint of Abdo Publishing | abdopublishing.com

CUTTING EDGE
SCIENCE +
TECHNOLOGY

abdopublishing.com

Published by Abdo Publishing, a division of ABDO, PO Box 398166, Minneapolis, Minnesota 55439. Copyright © 2016 by Abdo Consulting Group, Inc. International copyrights reserved in all countries. No part of this book may be reproduced in any form without written permission from the publisher. Essential Library™ is a trademark and logo of Abdo Publishing.

Printed in the United States of America, North Mankato, Minnesota
092015
012016

**THIS BOOK CONTAINS
RECYCLED MATERIALS**

Cover Photos: Gong Hangxu/iStockphoto, foreground; Belinda Images/SuperStock, background
Interior Photos: Transtock/Corbis, 4–5; iStockphoto, 8, 12, 15, 27, 28–29, 36–37, 40, 61, 82; Ringo H. W. Chiu/AP Images, 10; Red Line Editorial, 11; Simone Vieira/iStockphoto, 16–17; US Department of Energy, 18, 48; Monica Schroeder/Science Source, 19; Michael Bell/The Canadian Press/ AP Images, 21; Gary Hincks/Science Source, 23; Ron Thomas/iStockphoto, 25; Iano Andrade/AP Images, 31; Katsumi Kasahara/AP Images, 32; Yoshikazu Tsuno/AFP/Getty Images, 35; International Renewable Energy Agency, 39; Ethan Miller/Getty Images, 44–45; InterGary Tognoni/ iStockphoto, 46–47; Joshua Polson/The Greely Tribune/AP Images, 51; Altaeros/Rex Features/AP Images, 52 (top); Joseph Sohm/Shutterstock Images, 52 (bottom); CB2/ZOB/Supplied by WENN.com/Newscom, 53; Barry Batchelor/PA Wire/AP Images, 54; Patrick Pleul/Picture-Alliance/DPA/ AP Images, 57; Michael Utech/iStockphoto, 58–59, 78; Joao Abreu Miranda/AFP/Getty Images, 63; Steve Proehl/Proehl Studios/Corbis, 66; Kiyoshi Ota/Bloomberg/Getty Images, 68–69; Science Source, 71; Raupach/ullstein bild/Getty Images, 75; NASA, 76–77; David Guttenfelder/AP Images, 81; Enrico Sacchetti/Science Source, 85; ITER/Science Source, 87; Shutterstock Images, 88–89; Christopher Berkey/S&C Electric Company/AP Images, 91; Solent News/Rex Features/AP Images, 93; Steve Marcus/Reuters/Corbis, 94–95; Peter Dejong/AP Images, 96

Editor: Arnold Ringstad
Series Designer: Craig Hinton

Library of Congress Control Number: 2015945634

Cataloging-in-Publication Data
Hulick, Kathryn.
 Energy technology / Kathryn Hulick.
  p. cm. -- (Cutting-edge science and technology)
 ISBN 978-1-62403-915-7 (lib. bdg.)
 Includes bibliographical references and index.
 1. Renewable energy sources--Juvenile literature.   I. Title.
 333.79--dc23
                                                                      2015945634

CONTENTS

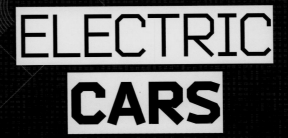

ONE

ELECTRIC CARS

A sleek silver sports car zips around a bend. Its engine does not roar. Instead it quietly whirs and whistles. The car has no tailpipe and produces no exhaust. Yet it can accelerate from 0 to 100 miles per hour (160 kmh) in seconds.[1] This is the Tesla Roadster, an electric car that runs on battery power. The futuristic car carries 6,831 battery cells packed together and plugs into any power outlet.[2] It can travel approximately 250 miles (400 km) on a full charge.[3] Electric vehicles (EVs) are just one of many cutting-edge technologies that are helping prepare the world to meet future energy needs.

In the 2010s, fossil fuels such as coal, oil, and natural gas powered the majority of our cars, trucks, homes, businesses, and factories. In 2011, these fuels supplied 81 percent of the world's energy.[4] However, the world cannot continue to rely on them. First, Earth has only a limited supply of these fuels. They are not renewable resources. Second, using fossil fuels is

Tesla Motors introduced the Roadster in 2008.

An Energy Pioneer

Tesla Motors named itself after Nikola Tesla, a Serbian inventor who worked in the late 1800s and early 1900s. Tesla developed the alternating current (AC) system of transmitting electricity. He famously feuded with American inventor Thomas Edison, who promoted direct current (DC) technology. In an AC system, the flow of electricity regularly changes direction. In a DC system, it goes one way. Tesla showed that AC was cheaper and more efficient, and most of the electricity we use today is delivered using AC. However, computers, electric cars, and other technologies still use DC.

Tesla filed for more than 700 patents, and his many inventions include wireless communications, remote controls, and turbines used in power generators. He also had ideas for harnessing solar energy and ocean energy.

harmful to the environment. Processing and burning fossil fuels creates pollution and contributes to climate change.

Many governments are investing in renewable energy technologies, which use resources that will always be available, such as sunlight, water, and wind. Renewable fuels such as biofuels are another option. These can be grown or harvested from plants or organic waste. Nuclear energy can also contribute to powering the future world. Scientists are working hard to make it safer and more efficient.

Electric cars will keep driving no matter which type of energy is used. Similar to laptops and cell phones, EVs run on batteries that need to be plugged in and recharged. The power flowing through the electric outlet could come from a coal-burning power plant, a nuclear reactor, solar panels, a wind farm, or any other power source. Because an EV does not produce any harmful fumes while driving, it will not pollute at all if it draws its electricity from clean power sources.

Driving on Batteries

In 2014, people in the United States purchased approximately 123,000 EVs. That's less than 1 percent of total car sales for the year, but it represents a big jump from EV sales in 2012, when only 52,600 of the cars were sold.[5] The cars are becoming more mainstream, and the auto industry has started paying closer attention to EVs. In 2013, the Tesla Model S became the first all-electric car to win the car of the year award from industry magazine *Motor Trend*. "In the future, I think there will be no gas stations," said Tesla CEO Elon Musk.[6] He believes everyone will drive electric cars.

However, a few important challenges remain before this future can become reality. Big battery packs increase the cost of the cars. The bigger the battery, the farther the car can go on one charge, but the more expensive it is. In addition, EV batteries typically take hours to recharge. In many locations, you cannot easily find a place to plug in a car if the battery dies. To overcome this issue, Tesla is building stations throughout the country where a driver can quickly charge the battery using a high-powered electricity source.

◄ Power Plant Pollution

EV batteries are charged using electricity from the grid, which usually gets its power from fossil fuels such as coal or natural gas. How is that any different from burning the gas in the car itself? Power plants are much more efficient than a car's engine. They can harvest more energy from fuel than a car can. They can also capture heat that gets produced while burning the fuel and use it to produce additional power. This heat gets wasted in a car's engine. Elon Musk, the founder of Tesla Motors, explains that a power plant generating electricity from natural gas can reach approximately 60 percent efficiency.[7] This means 60 percent of the energy the plant generates gets used as electricity. "If you put that same fuel in an internal combustion engine car, you get about 20 percent efficiency," he said.[8]

EVs have seen a dramatic increase in popularity.

Researchers are working hard to develop batteries that are cheaper, more powerful, and quicker to recharge, but big breakthroughs are rare. Instead, engineers keep making small improvements to current battery technology. Most EVs today use lithium-ion batteries. This same technology powers devices such as cameras, cell phones, and laptop computers. In the current Tesla Model S, rows of lithium-ion battery cells take up most of the space in the floor of the car between the front and rear wheels.

Another way to improve any type of energy technology is to increase efficiency. Redesigning the shape and size of a wind turbine or solar panel can increase the amount of energy it produces. Likewise, redesigning an electric car can decrease the amount of energy it needs to run. A light, sleek car is more energy efficient than a heavy one. A lower weight means it takes less battery power to propel the car forward. A sleek design reduces drag from the surrounding air.

Tesla designed the Roadster and Model S with these facts in mind. Most cars are built with a heavy steel body, but the Roadster is made of carbon fiber. This material is expensive, but it is much lighter than steel and has comparable strength. The Model S is mostly aluminum, another light but strong metal. Musk also runs the rocket company SpaceX, and he has used some of his space technology in his cars: "We applied a lot of rocket design techniques to make the car light despite having a very large battery pack."[9]

◢ **Hybrids**

Hybrid EVs run on either electricity or gas. This offers a solution to drivers who do not want to have to stop often to charge the battery or who worry about getting stranded in a place with no charging station nearby. A typical hybrid contains an internal combustion engine along with a battery pack and electric motor. Most hybrids do not need to be plugged in. The combustion engine recharges the battery, and the electric motor helps capture energy generated by braking. Hybrids conserve fuel by automatically shutting off the gas engine when the car comes to a stop. Computers in these cars determine the best times to switch between the gasoline and electric modes.

New Ways to Power Up

Whereas some researchers are trying to build cheap, powerful batteries that last a long time, others are looking into different methods of powering an electric engine. Supercapacitors, also known as

Elon **Musk**
(1971–)

Elon Musk thinks about big problems. "When I was in university, I thought about, what are the problems that are most likely to affect the future of the world or the future of humanity?"[10] he said. He decided it was extremely important to have sustainable energy and transportation so civilization as we know it can continue to progress. Musk has certainly reached that goal. His company Tesla Motors makes electric cars; SpaceX sends rockets into space; and SolarCity, where he is chairman of the board, develops solar energy.

Growing up in South Africa, Musk was bullied at school. But that did not stop him from dreaming. He founded the company that became PayPal, a service that helps people send money online. Musk made a fortune when Internet auction site eBay bought PayPal for $1.5 billion in 2002.[11] He poured his money into space travel and electric cars. Since then, his vision has transformed both industries. Tesla's cars have won numerous awards and the company has developed improved battery technology. SpaceX reduced the cost of rocket travel and won a contract to send astronauts to the International Space Station.

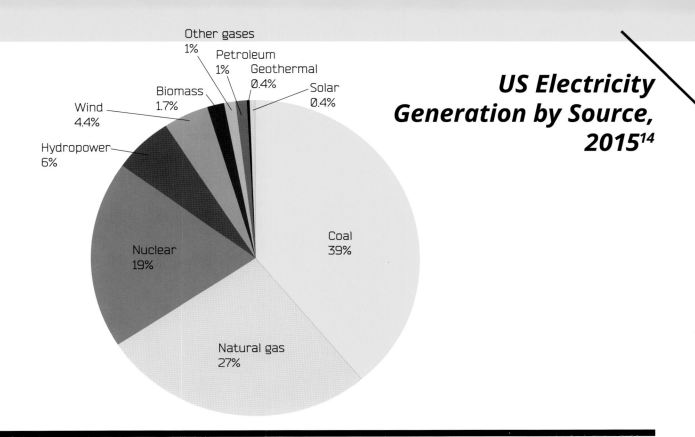

Other gases
1%

Petroleum
1%

Geothermal
0.4%

Solar
0.4%

Biomass
1.7%

Wind
4.4%

Hydropower
6%

Nuclear
19%

Coal
39%

Natural gas
27%

ultracapacitors, are similar to rechargeable batteries. Both technologies store and release electricity. The difference is that capacitors recharge extremely quickly—in as little as 16 seconds.[12] The problem is that a supercapacitor has to be much larger than a battery to hold the same amount of energy. If researchers find a way to reduce their size and cost, they could prove useful for EVs.

Hydrogen fuel cells are another technology that can power electric cars. A fuel cell combines hydrogen gas with oxygen from the air to make electricity. This chemical reaction gives off water and heat, so it does not pollute the air. Instead of plugging in the car to recharge, drivers pump in hydrogen gas. Some prototypes can travel approximately 300 miles (480 km) before refueling.[13]

In 2007, General Motors provided seven interested and enthusiastic people with fuel cell cars to drive for free as a test of the technology. One of the drivers said, "We feel like we're contributing to something important, to drive a car with no gasoline that contributes nothing to pollution and global warming."[15] She won her spot after participating in General Motors' online forums discussing fuel cell vehicles. Toyota, Honda, and Hyundai all planned to begin selling fuel cell vehicles to the public starting in 2015 and 2016.

Cheap and Efficient

EVs are cleaner than gas-powered cars, whether they are powered by batteries, supercapacitors, fuel cells, or some other technology that has not been imagined yet. However, people need energy for much more than only transportation.

Our civilization requires a steady supply of fuel and electricity. To get electricity, we rely on a network of power lines, stations, and power plants. This infrastructure is known as the electric grid. In the coming decades, climate change and a dwindling supply of fossil fuels will lead to a change in the types of energy we rely on. Researchers and engineers are working to come up with the energy technologies for tomorrow.

To hasten the speed of this change, new energy technology will need to be cheap and efficient enough to compete with fossil fuels. No matter how innovative a new source of energy may be, it is unlikely to enter widespread use unless it produces a large amount of power at a low cost. Gas-powered cars continue to outsell electric ones for the simple reason that they are cheaper and more convenient to refuel.

The race is on to produce clean, sustainable energy for an affordable price. The contenders to replace fossil fuels include biofuels, hydrogen, solar, wind, water, nuclear fission, and nuclear fusion. The future may not belong to a single winner among these options. Instead, it is more likely a mix of these new energy sources will power the world.

Auto manufacturer Hyundai showed off its latest hydrogen fuel cell engine at a car show in 2015.

TWO

FOSSIL FUELS

The gasoline in your car's tank, the natural gas heating your home, and the coal that burns in a local power plant all come from beneath the surface of the earth. Fossil fuels are made from the remains of ancient animals and plants compressed for hundreds of millions of years. Ancient water animals buried at the bottom of an ocean or river eventually decompose and turn into petroleum. This thick, gooey substance is also called crude oil. In deeper, hotter places inside the earth, these ancient animals became natural gas instead.

Fossil fuels have been abundant and cheap for decades. But as people use up Earth's natural stores, they could become rare and expensive. They are also controversial, because extracting and burning them can harm the environment. A few of the dangers of fossil fuels include climate change, oil spills, acid rain, earthquakes, and pollution. Most governments and experts agree we need to transition toward renewable,

Retrieving fossil fuels from underground or under water often requires complex, expensive equipment.

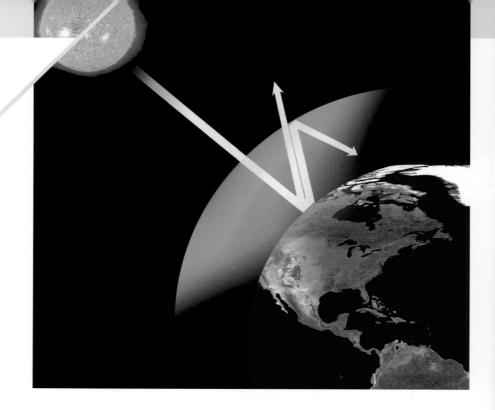

Once released into the atmosphere, the gases produced by fossil fuel consumption help block some of the sun's energy from reflecting back into space.

environmentally friendly sources of energy. At the same time, they argue that while we continue using fossil fuels, we should develop new technologies to burn them more cleanly. "We're heading into an era where if we don't change what we're doing, we're going to be fundamentally in really deep trouble," said US Secretary of Energy Steven Chu.[1]

The Greenhouse Effect

Carbon is a chemical element found inside the cells and tissues of living things. Fossil fuels, which are formed from the remains of living things, contain concentrated carbon or carbon compounds. When people burn these fuels, carbon dioxide is released from those compounds into the air. Natural levels of carbon dioxide in the air are not a problem. Plants need this gas to live. But for the past several decades, human machines and factories have spewed out more and more carbon dioxide. At the same time, people have cut down forests that help remove carbon dioxide from the air. These human activities have changed the chemical composition of Earth's atmosphere. Carbon dioxide and other gases, known as greenhouse gases, trap heat in the atmosphere. This phenomenon is known as the greenhouse effect.

Steven **Chu**
(1948–)

Steven Chu served as the US Secretary of Energy from 2009 to 2013. In 2010, an explosion on the Deepwater Horizon oil rig sent oil gushing into the Gulf of Mexico for five months. Chu led a team of scientists that helped figure out how to cap the well and stop the spill. The disaster made the public aware of the dangers of fossil fuels and the need to find renewable energy replacements.

Under Chu's leadership, the US Department of Energy provided billions of dollars to support clean-energy research, ranging from solar cells and wind farms to electric car batteries. Chu is a scientist first and a politician second. In fact, he has a Nobel Prize in Physics for his work using lasers to cool and trap atoms. His heroes when he was growing up included Isaac Newton and Albert Einstein.

Similar to many other prominent scientists, Chu is concerned about climate change. In Chu's opinion, researchers will find new ways to keep extracting more fossil fuels, providing a steady supply that will not run out for a long time. But if we keep relying on these fuels, we could cause lasting damage to our planet. He thinks we need to begin a new era of renewable energy. "The Stone Age did not end because we ran out of stones," he said. "We transitioned to better solutions."[2]

◢ Clean Coal?

In 2014, SaskPower in Canada opened the first coal-fired power plant to use carbon capture and storage (CCS) technology on a large scale. The exhaust from the burning coal gets sent through a chemical process that isolates the carbon dioxide and converts it into a liquid form. SaskPower sends some of the captured carbon dioxide to a nearby oil field to help extract more oil. The rest gets pumped far underground. Good sites for carbon storage contain rocks with many small, interconnected holes to hold the carbon dioxide. Some risks are associated with CCS. For example, the accidental release of the stored carbon dioxide can be hazardous to groundwater.

CCS helps protect the environment, but it comes at a cost. Now, 20 percent of the electricity SaskPower produces goes toward capturing carbon.[4] The plant may be less efficient, but the new technology will reduce the plant's emissions by approximately 90 percent each year. That is equal to taking 250,000 cars off the road.[5]

This runaway greenhouse effect leads to climate change. By the 2010s, it had already caused noticeable effects, including melting ice caps and warmer global temperatures. In the future, it could cause sea levels to rise, storms to become more common, and many plants and animals to go extinct.

One way to limit the effects of climate change is to reduce carbon dioxide emissions. New sources of renewable energy are key to a long-term solution. In the short term, though, researchers are finding ways to reduce emissions from our current energy sources. For example, manufacturers are designing appliances and vehicles that use energy more efficiently.

In addition, carbon capture technologies can prevent carbon dioxide from entering the atmosphere. "We need to develop the technologies that enable us to use our fossil fuels in a clean way," said Chu. "It will take a half century to get our carbon emissions down to where we need to go to protect the climate."[3]

A new carbon capture facility opened in Saskatoon, Canada, in October 2014.

Running on Empty

Fossil fuels power the modern world. Each day, people in the United States use 20 million barrels of oil. More than half of that oil powers transportation, including cars, freight trucks, and airplanes.[6] The majority of the world's electricity comes from coal-burning and natural gas power plants. China approved the construction of 15 new, large-scale coal mines in 2013.[7] In the United States in 2014, coal provided 39 percent of the country's electric power. Natural gas contributed another 27 percent.[8]

However, Earth is running out of fossil fuels. One estimate says that there are enough oil and natural gas reserves to meet global demand for approximately 50 more years.[9] Coal is more plentiful and could last 112 years.[10] After that time, supplies could start dwindling. However, these estimates count only fossil fuel deposits that people know about and can access with current mining and drilling technology. It is possible geologists could discover new deposits of fuel or find new ways to extract them. In fact, this is exactly what happened during a natural gas boom in the United States in the early 2000s. A technology known as fracking made it possible to retrieve more fossil fuels from underground, although it attracted considerable controversy.

A Fracking Frenzy

Fracking is short for hydraulic fracturing, a technique that uses water, sand, and chemicals to crack rocks as deep as 10,000 feet (3,000 m) below Earth's surface.[11] Once the rocks are broken, drilling can extract trapped reserves of natural gas or oil. Huge shale rock formations stretch across much of the United

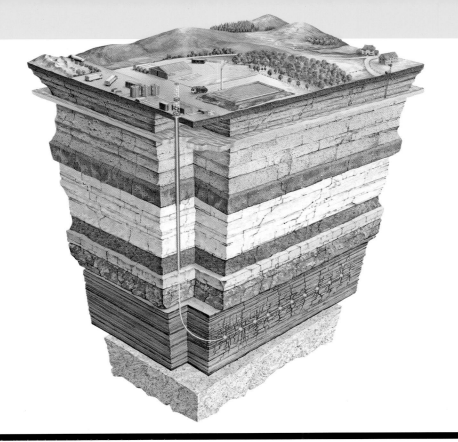

How Fracking Works

In the process of fracking, workers pump fluids far below the surface. These fluids then travel in horizontal wells through shale deposits. Shale is a type of rock made up of compacted layers of clay and minerals. The fluids form cracks in the shale. Sand is pumped through the well to keep these cracks open while natural gas flows out and is brought to the surface.

States, but until recently, engineers did not have a good way to extract fuel from them. Shale rock was considered too hard to crack. The company Mitchell Energy made a big breakthrough in 1997 when it experimented with a new fracking fluid, sometimes called slick water. The mixture flowed faster than previously used fluids.

At the same time, engineers were perfecting a method of horizontal drilling. A typical oil or gas well goes straight down into the ground, right through the middle of a rock formation. Wells using horizontal drilling are dug sideways, allowing companies to extract much more gas from one well.

Three-Dimensional Seismic Imaging

Three-dimensional seismic imaging allows oil companies to map rock formations thousands of feet below the surface of the earth. The maps show them exactly where to drill to establish a successful well.

To perform seismic imaging, a survey team sets up devices called geophones along the surface. Then, the team uses large trucks or buried explosives to make vibrations. These travel through the ground and bounce off layers of buried rock. The geophones collect the reflected vibrations, and then computers analyze the data to build maps.

To get a three-dimensional picture of the rock formations, the team must gather data from thousands of locations. In 1972, the energy company Exxon did a three-dimensional seismic survey, but it took two years for the computers of that time period to process a month's data.[14] Now, computer technology has advanced dramatically, and oil companies can make three-dimensional maps more quickly and cheaply than ever before.

Together, horizontal drilling and fracking made it possible to tap into the United States' shale rock formations. However, it is fruitless to drill for gas unless the driller knows where to put the well. Technological advancements in seismic imaging, or using sound waves to look through rocks, made it possible to map out deep shale formations in three dimensions. All of these advances set off a huge boom in US fossil fuel production.

Deep Danger

Fracking has many benefits, but it is also controversial. During a fracking operation, as many as 5 million gallons (19 million L) of water get pumped down one well.[13] That is equal to 400 to 600 full tanker trucks. But only 200 to 300 trucks carry wastewater away from the well afterward. This means that one-half of the fluid remains underground. Many people argue it can contaminate groundwater. In the 2011 documentary *Gasland*, a man turns on the tap in his kitchen then holds a lighter to the water, and

Natural gas power plants burn fossil fuels, resulting in high-pressure gas that spins a turbine and generates electricity.

it catches fire. Activists contended that flammable gas from a nearby fracking operation had contaminated the water supply. Many families living near oil and gas rigs have complained of problems with their water and their health. Fracking and the disposal of fracking wastewater have also both been linked to earthquakes because of the pressure they put on faults.

Despite these dangers, natural gas will likely provide most of our electric power in the near future. Natural gas can also supply transportation fuel. Some trucking companies are already outfitting their vehicles to run on liquefied natural gas. In addition, the gas can be processed to produce biofuels that can replace gasoline or hydrogen that can power fuel cells.

Natural gas power plants produce one-half as much pollution as coal-fired plants, but renewable energy sources such as solar, wind, water, and geothermal are much cleaner options.[15] Unfortunately, producing energy from these sources is usually more expensive than using fossil fuels. Researchers are working hard to improve renewable energy technology with hope that one day we will not need to rely on fossil fuels any longer.

THREE

RENEWABLE FUEL

Fossil fuels form when plant or animal matter gets compressed for millions of years. However, they are not the only source of fuel created from living things. Factories can process biomass to produce a variety of biofuels. In fact, most of the gasoline available in the United States today contains 10 percent ethanol, made from corn.[1] And in Brazil, the efforts of government leaders, including former president Luiz Inácio Lula da Silva, have led to every gas station offering sugarcane-based ethanol fuel in addition to regular gasoline.

Burning any plant- or animal-based fuel produces greenhouse gases such as carbon dioxide. However, biofuels come from plants and animals living now, not millions of years ago. As plants grow, they absorb carbon dioxide. Burning fuel made from newly harvested plants puts gases that were recently absorbed back into the air. The total amount of carbon dioxide in the

Sorghum is one of many crops used to create biofuels.

environment does not change. For this reason, biofuels are more environmentally friendly than fossil fuels, and they provide a safer, cleaner alternative.

From Algae to Turkey Guts

Biofuels are renewable, but they have an impact on limited resources such as land and water. Growing sugarcane or corn for biofuels uses farmland that could produce food to eat. These crops also use freshwater, which is scarce in many areas. Researchers have come up with a range of alternatives to biofuels made from food crops.

◢ Algae Farms

Algae reproduce very quickly. A colony can double its size in as little as six hours.[2] This quick reproductive rate enables scientists to modify the algae's genetic code between generations, altering the way a species grows and how it behaves. It could be possible to engineer a new form of algae that produces usable fuel without the need for special processing. "We just have to combine [genes] in a way that nature has not done before. We're speeding up evolution by billions of years," said genetic researcher J. Craig Venter, founder of a not-for-profit research organization.[3] The environmental impact of these rapid changes, if any, is unknown.

Algae are one promising source for biofuels. These single-celled plants grow in freshwater or salt water. They can be converted into various forms and burned to release energy. Algae do not take up farmland, and they can often feed on or even clean contaminated wastewater. A family of desert plants, halophytes, can also thrive on wastewater or salt water. The aircraft company Boeing and the Sustainable Bioenergy Research Consortium (SBRC) in the United Arab Emirates have been experimenting with using these plants for fuel. Scientists at SBRC are planting halophytes in sandy desert soil and using salty wastewater from a nearby fish and shrimp farm to feed the plants. The farm will produce both edible food

Luiz Inácio Lula **da Silva**

(1945–)

Luiz Inácio Lula da Silva served as president of Brazil from 2003 through 2011. He started working at a young age to help support his family. In the 1970s, he fought for workers' rights and even served prison time after organizing a series of strikes.

During his presidency, Brazil's economy boomed and the country achieved energy independence, meaning it produced enough fuel to meet all of its own energy needs. Brazil began this path in 1975, when it started replacing oil with ethanol made from sugarcane. Da Silva's administration helped the country switch to flex-fuel cars, which can handle pure gasoline or ethanol fuel, or any mix of the two. "We wanted to make sure we could produce our own fuel, and that we were able to have a less polluting fuel," said da Silva.[4] "As time goes by, Brazil is proving that biofuel is an extraordinary alternative. And slowly the countries will be convinced," da Silva said. "We have to invest in alternative fuels. The world needs this."[5]

31

Japan Airlines carried out test flights with a blend of biofuel and normal jet fuel in 2009.

and fuel. Boeing is looking into other biofuels as well. In 2014, the company made the world's first flight using only diesel jet fuel made from algae.

Other companies are taking different approaches to renewable fuels. Changing World Technologies showed it is possible to convert any type of carbon-based material, from plastic to animal parts, into a diesel fuel called biocrude. The company used intense heat and pressure to break apart the molecules that make up the waste. This is similar to the natural process that happens inside Earth to produce fossil fuels, but in a factory it can be done in less than an hour.[6] The company built a facility in Missouri that processed turkey guts. However, the fuel was not high quality, and the company could not sell very much of it. Changing World Technologies went bankrupt, but other organizations and individuals are successfully converting grease and used cooking oil from restaurants into biodiesel.

Harnessing Hydrogen

Whereas some researchers focus on renewable forms of oil and gasoline to feed combustion engines, others want to move toward hydrogen. Hydrogen fuel could provide the energy of the future. Hydrogen is the simplest and most common element in the universe. Fuel cell technology can convert hydrogen into electricity. The only emission is water.

But making hydrogen fuel can be tricky. The element is most often trapped within compounds, such as water or gases. Factories have to extract the hydrogen from these compounds using intense heat or other methods. Today, a technology called natural gas reforming provides 95 percent of the hydrogen produced in the United States.[7] This process starts

◄ How Does a Fuel Cell Work?

Fuel cell technology uses a chemical reaction to produce electricity. Most fuel cells take hydrogen fuel, but the cells can be constructed to run on other fuels as well. The hydrogen fuel cell process is cleaner and more efficient than a combustion engine. In fact, a fuel cell is more similar to a battery than an engine. Like a battery, a fuel cell has a negative side and a positive side. Hydrogen fuel feeds into one side, where another chemical called a catalyst causes electrons to separate from the hydrogen atoms. These electrons supply electricity. At the same time, oxygen from the air comes in through the other side and joins with the leftover hydrogen to form water.

Fuel Cell Power

Most fuel cells operating today are not found in cars. Instead, they power whole buildings. In the United States, some universities, hospitals, and data centers get their electricity from large, stationary fuel cells. This type of fuel cell can also provide electricity during power outages. During Hurricane Sandy in 2012, cell phone towers in New York, New Jersey, and Connecticut kept running thanks to fuel cell back-up systems. In South Korea, a fuel cell power plant provides electricity and heat to nearby homes.

Some stationary fuel cells operate at very high temperatures that would not be safe inside a car. They are known as molten carbonate or solid oxide fuel cells. They convert fuel to electricity and produce a lot of extra heat in the process. This heat can power a generator to produce even more electricity.

with natural gas, which is a fossil fuel. So although the fuel cells themselves do not produce any pollution or emissions, creating the hydrogen to run the fuel cells involves burning normal fossil fuels, indirectly causing pollution.

However, researchers are working on a variety of methods to cleanly produce hydrogen. A technique called electrolysis separates hydrogen from water using electricity, and that electric power could come from a renewable energy source.

Other techniques take advantage of special types of bacteria or other biological processes to break down biomass and produce hydrogen. For example, researchers at Virginia Tech found a way to separate hydrogen from corn husks and stalks. "We believe this exciting technology has the potential to enable the widespread use of hydrogen fuel cell vehicles around the world and displace fossil fuels," said Joe Rollin, who led the research.[8]

Japanese technology giant Toshiba built a facility that uses electrolysis to generate mass quantities of hydrogen.

FOUR

SOLAR POWER

We live on a solar-powered planet. Plants take in energy from the sun and convert it to the food they need to grow. When animals eat those plants or get eaten themselves, that energy is passed up the food chain. The sunlight that strikes Earth in only one hour contains enough energy to meet humanity's needs for an entire year. We only have to learn how to harvest it.

Solar panels can turn sunlight into electricity, but the limitations of the technology mean solar energy currently supplies less than one-tenth of 1 percent of the world's energy needs.[1] Researchers are working hard to find cheaper, more efficient ways to capture solar energy.

Elon Musk chairs the company SolarCity, which installs solar panels. He is confident this company and others will succeed in making solar energy a major power source within 20 years. "I'm quite confident that the primary means of power generation

Solar panels are one of the most direct tools for turning sunlight into usable electricity.

will be solar," he said. "We've got this giant fusion generator in the sky called the sun, and we just need to tap a little bit of that energy for purposes of human civilization."[2]

Solar Everywhere

Imagine a world where see-through solar panels cover every window, providing electricity for buildings. Sunlight could also power up the battery of a mobile device without the need for an electric outlet. Researchers are working on big ideas like these. One roadblock standing in the way of an entirely solar-powered city or country is cost.

Solar panels are expensive to produce, install, and maintain, though the cost has been dropping rapidly for the past decade. The US Department of Energy introduced a program called SunShot in 2011 with the goal of bringing the price of solar energy down. The program provides money to researchers and companies working on solar technology.

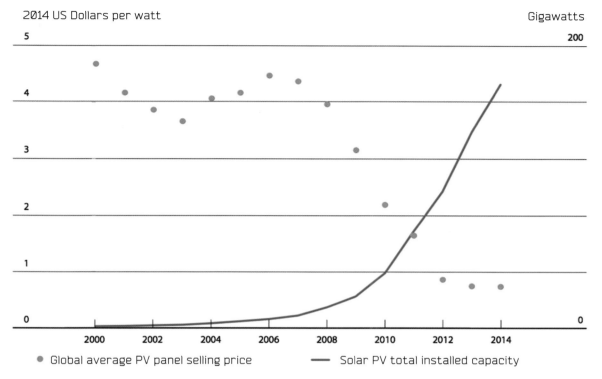

2014 US Dollars per watt

Gigawatts

Since the year 2000, the cost of solar panels has dropped dramatically. This drop has been accompanied by a rise in the installed capacity of US solar power.

● Global average PV panel selling price   — Solar PV total installed capacity

Taming Sunlight

Most solar panels are made up of many small photovoltaic (PV) solar cells. PV solar cells convert sunlight directly into electricity. They can do this thanks to the photoelectric effect, which is a chemical property of some materials. When sunlight hits this type of material, it releases electrons. Feeding those electrons into a wire creates electric current.

Panels in fixed positions on rooftops only operate at peak efficiency when the sun shines directly on them.

Crystalline silicon is the most popular material for PV solar cells because it typically provides the best efficiency for its cost. In the lab, silicon cells can convert 25 percent of the light that hits them into electricity. However, this performance is impossible to match on a rooftop, where conditions, including weather and the angle of the sun, are never ideal. On a rooftop, a typical solar panel reaches 15 to 18 percent efficiency.[5]

◢ Thin and Versatile

Thin-film PV cells take 100 times less material to absorb the same amount of sunlight as in a traditional cell.[8] The thinner, lighter size of this new technology makes it more versatile than big, bulky panels. The new cells could be paired with electronic devices or layered over roof shingles or windows. However, it is difficult to mass-produce thin-film cells that are as efficient as the larger silicon ones.

Many technologies are competing to reach better efficiency or a lower cost than silicon solar cells. One promising avenue of research is concentrating PV technology, which uses mirrors to focus sunlight on a small group of highly efficient cells. Another method is thin-film PV technology, which uses a very thin layer of photoelectric materials applied over glass or metal. Some researchers are working on transparent solar cells or solar coatings. An invisible layer of solar material could cover a window or device screen to provide power without anyone noticing it is there.

Recently, a material called perovskite has inspired excitement in the PV industry. This mineral is cheap and easy to work with, and it absorbs more of the light spectrum than silicon does. "You can put perovskite on top of traditional silicon cells to make them more efficient," said Michael Graetzel of the Federal Institute of Technology in Switzerland.[6] Researchers around the globe are working with this material, and a team at Stanford University believes it will help boost solar cell efficiency to as high as 30 percent in the next five to ten years.[7]

A Forest of Mirrors

PV solar cells are a direct way to turn sunlight into electricity. Another method, called solar thermal power, uses the sun as a source of heat to boil water to produce steam. The steam then turns a turbine to generate electricity. The largest solar power plant in the world, the Ivanpah Solar Electric Generating System, opened in January 2014 in the Mojave Desert in California. The plant looks like a forest of mirrors surrounding a tall, central tower. The mirrors are mounted onto 173,500 heliostats.[9] The heliostats focus the sun's rays onto the tower, which is full of water. The plant produces enough electricity to power 140,000 homes.[10]

Other solar thermal power plants use rows of curved mirrors to focus sunlight onto pipes full of synthetic oil. At the Solana plant in Arizona, which opened in 2013, the hot oil can go in two directions. It either heats water to create steam for generating electricity, or it heats tanks full of molten salt. This liquid salt can store heat energy for up to six hours.[11]

◢ Clear as Day

Solar cells need to trap light to work, but a transparent one has to let light through. Researchers at the Massachusetts Institute of Technology (MIT) solved this problem using materials that let visible light through but absorb ultraviolet and infrared light. "A honey bee—which sees in the ultraviolet—wouldn't think it's transparent, but we humans do," said Vladimir Bulović of MIT.[12] The team has used an array of their invisible solar cells to power the display on a small clock. Right now the technology only has 2 percent efficiency, but the team believes it can reach 12 percent by improving the design.[13] Eventually, coatings applied over windows could provide all or most of the energy needs of a home or skyscraper.

When the Sun Does Not Shine

Solana's ability to store solar heat for later is very important. Power is needed at all hours of the day, but the sun is an intermittent energy source, meaning it does not always shine. At night or on cloudy days, a solar power plant or solar panel will not generate any electricity directly from the sun. People relying on solar energy either need a back-up energy source or a way to store energy for later. After cost and efficiency, intermittency is the third big challenge to any solar power technology.

Most solar energy systems installed on homes and businesses today are hooked up to the electric grid, and power can flow both ways. The owner of the building typically gets paid for any extra electricity the solar panels produce but still has to buy the electricity he or she uses when the sun is not shining. This electricity often comes from power plants that burn fossil fuels. Batteries and other storage systems can let people use their solar energy off the grid entirely. They remove any need for electricity that was produced using coal or gas. However, batteries are large and expensive. Some electricity is lost when transferring power to and from them. Advances in batteries may help intermittent energy sources become more attractive.

Whereas many researchers focus on reducing the cost and improving the efficiency of solar cells, others are working on new ideas for solar power storage. As long as innovators around the world are focusing on solar energy, the future outlook for this type of renewable energy remains bright.

SHARPER
FOCUS

If you have ever experimented with a magnifying glass, you know it is easy to focus sunlight to burn a hole through a leaf. This simple effect can help increase the amount of power any type of solar technology produces. Solar thermal power plants rely on mirrors that focus sunlight to generate heat. Solar cells can benefit from concentrated sunlight, too. Concentrating photovoltaic (CPV) technology is more efficient than silicon or thin-film PV cells, but it usually costs more because it requires special mirrors.

An IBM team announced in 2014 it had constructed a CPV system that reaches an impressive 80 percent efficiency and amplifies sunlight to 2,000 times its usual intensity.[14] The device uses a tracking system to aim a large mirrored dish toward the sun. The dish reflects almost all of the incoming light onto hundreds of 0.16-square-inch (1 sq cm) PV chips.[15] Cooling liquid protects the chips from melting in the intense beam.

Though the Ivanpah plant produces clean energy, the extremely high air temperatures it produces have proven deadly to hundreds of birds flying between the mirrors and the tower.

FIVE

WIND ENERGY

If you have ever ridden on a sailboat, you have experienced the power of wind energy. The wind flowing across the sail creates lift, which pushes the sailboat through the water. The same principle powers thousands of wind turbines throughout the world. Wind is a renewable resource, and it can provide electricity without using up fuel or causing pollution. Between 2008 and 2013, wind power use in the United States tripled.[1] The country now gets approximately 4.4 percent of its electricity from wind, compared with only 0.4 percent from solar energy.[2]

Wind energy is usually cheaper and more efficient than solar power. A wind turbine converts between 20 and 40 percent of the energy from wind into electricity.[3] Home solar panels typically have an efficiency of approximately 15 percent.[4] However, wind energy also comes with challenges. Wind turbines take up a lot of space, and, like solar, wind is an intermittent energy source. The wind doesn't blow all the time, and

Companies in the United States have constructed many vast wind farms in recent years.

Wind Turbine

A modern wind turbine is a complex machine designed to maximize electricity output while maintaining safety. Yaw and pitch systems ensure the blades are oriented in the optimal direction. A tall tower structure places the blades at a high enough altitude to take advantage of strong winds. A brake slows the turbine if it approaches unsafe speeds.

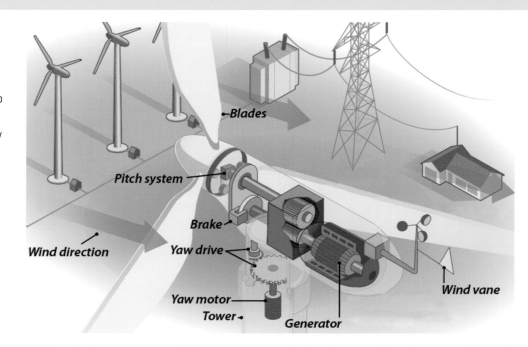

some places are windier than others. Wind turbines are getting smarter with the help of sensors and computer technology that make automatic adjustments based on current wind conditions. Researchers are also working on totally new designs for wind turbines and enhancements to current technology that improve reliability and efficiency.

Bigger and Taller

The most common type of modern wind turbine looks like an airplane propeller attached to the top of a tall pole. In fact, a turbine's blades are each shaped like an airplane's wing. Air flows unevenly around them, generating lift against the back and drag against the front. This makes them spin. The spinning motion runs a generator that produces electric current.

Taller Towers

Building very tall towers can be an expensive, tricky feat of engineering. One problem is that manufacturers have to ship the pieces of a turbine to the wind farm where it will be assembled. If the pieces are too big, trucks cannot safely carry them on regular roads. In the United States, the tallest towers reach approximately 260 feet tall (79 m).[8]

The company Keystone Power Systems offers a solution: construct the tower on-site using spiral welding. If you cut open a cardboard paper towel tube along the seam, you will see that it is made from a flat piece of cardboard rolled up. Keystone rolls and welds flat metal sheets in a similar way to make towers 400 feet (120 m) tall or higher. At that height, the turbine reaches above any trees that might block the wind. Eric Smith, one of the company's founders, said, "Once you're at the heights we're looking at, it really opens up the whole country for turbines to capture large amounts of energy."[9]

Bigger is better when it comes to wind turbines. Longer blades can capture more wind. In addition, the wind blows most strongly higher up in the atmosphere. Far above the tallest turbines, at tens of thousands of feet, the available energy from high-altitude winds could provide 100 times the amount of electricity that the world needs.[5] Some engineers have looked to the sky for power, designing airborne turbines that float or fly to harness this energy source. These are not yet in widespread use, but some are in the testing phases.

The company Vestas broke the record for the largest working wind turbine in 2014 when it built a prototype of its V164 turbine. It is 722 feet (220 m) tall, and each blade is 262 feet (80 m) long.[6] One of these turbines can produce enough energy to power 7,500 homes each year. "We haven't hit the barrier yet for how large these machines can be," said Paul Veers of the National Renewable Energy Laboratory.[7] He predicts that they will continue getting bigger and taller.

Ocean Winds

The blades on modern turbines are built to enormous sizes.

Most wind farms operating today stand in fields or on hilltops, but engineers are also building wind turbines at sea. Vestas designed the V164 to work in the ocean. The wind blows more strongly over the ocean than over land, so offshore wind farms have the potential to produce a lot of energy. However, these farms are also more expensive to build, and it can be difficult to connect them to the electric grid on land. Engineers are working to solve these problems. More than 70 offshore wind farms are currently operating, mostly in Europe.[10]

The largest offshore wind farm in the world, the London Array, opened in July 2013 with 175 turbines. The United Kingdom's prime minister, David Cameron, called the project "a big win for renewable energy." The turbines provide power to 500,000 homes.[11]

Engineers can build very large wind turbines at sea because they can bring in the parts they need on ships. On land, the width of roads limits the size of parts that can be transported.

◢ Floating Energy

One way to reach the fastest winds high up in the sky is to build a very tall tower. Another way is to design something that floats or flies, and engineers have built turbines that do just that. The company Makani Power builds a kitelike turbine that flies 1,000 feet (300 m) in the air. The kite's wings are very similar to the blades of a regular turbine, and it sends electricity down a tether to the ground. A typical turbine tower made of steel may weigh more than 100 short tons (90 metric tons), whereas Makani's airborne turbine design weighs one-tenth as much and costs much less.[12]

HOW TO
CAPTURE WIND

A tall wind turbine with two or three propeller-like blades may be the most popular design, but it is certainly not the only way to capture wind. Researchers have come up with many clever, cool, and outlandish ideas for new ways to harness wind energy.

BUOYANT AIRBORNE TURBINE

Altaeros Energies developed the buoyant airborne turbine, a blimp-like turbine, and tested it over Alaska. The company plans to deploy it in places such as disaster areas or remote villages where electricity is not readily available.

VERTICAL-AXIS WIND TURBINE

Vertical-axis wind turbines (VAWTs) typically look more like eggbeaters than propellers.

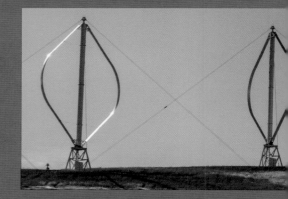

No one has yet built one of these turbines that can top a regular horizontal turbine's efficiency, but engineers keep trying. Sandia National Laboratories has been testing very large VAWTs for possible use at sea.

Though the so-called strawscraper was not actually built, artist's renderings were created as part of the conceptual study.

STRAWSCRAPER

An architectural company in Sweden came up with a concept to cover an entire skyscraper in Stockholm, the nation's capital, with threads of material that generate an electric charge when they rub together in the wind.

Wind farms have drawn more public protests than most other forms of renewable power.

Environmental Impacts

Though wind turbines produce clean energy, they can also have negative effects. They take up a large amount of land relative to the quantity of energy they generate, because the turbines must be spaced widely apart to be effective. Turbines can also be harmful to wildlife. Scientists have studied bird and bat deaths caused by collisions with the spinning blades of turbines. However, relatively few of these deaths occur, and experts are working to reduce this effect.

Some people oppose the construction of wind farms near their homes. They may oppose the sound and vibration caused by fast-spinning turbines. Engineers are developing new blade materials that will minimize these issues. Other people living near wind turbines believe the large structures disrupt the natural environment. Companies that build wind farms often consult with nearby residents to ensure their facilities cause as little disruption to communities as possible.

Reading the Air

Wind regularly changes both in direction and intensity. Current wind turbines have control systems that automatically adjust to wind conditions. For example, a pitch adjustment changes the angle of the blades, which can help keep them spinning at approximately the same rate no matter how fast the wind is blowing. A yaw adjustment rotates the entire head of the wind turbine to face into the wind. Extremely fast wind can damage a turbine, so it will turn off in high winds and turn on again when the wind is at a more favorable speed.

Researchers are working on smart technologies that will improve these control systems. For example, some have proposed adding flaps with sensors to the edge of a turbine blade. These flaps could monitor air flow and make tiny adjustments to improve the aerodynamics of the blade, enhancing its ability to cut through the air efficiently.

The intermittency of wind can also cause problems for the electric grid. If a wind farm suddenly dumps a huge amount of power into the grid, it could overload the grid and cause a blackout. Or, if the turbines don't produce any electricity for a couple of hours, another source of power has to fill the gap. Power utility companies may keep back-up power plants idling, ready to jump in if the wind stops blowing. An idling coal or gas power plant wastes energy and produces pollution.

Smart technology offers a solution to this problem. Sensors on the turbines in a Colorado wind farm constantly record the wind speed and send this data along to powerful computers every five minutes. These same computers also receive data from weather satellites and other wind farms. Programs use artificial intelligence to process all of this information and generate extremely accurate predictions of future wind conditions. Electric utility companies can then plan ahead for periods of very high or very low energy output. In the future, advanced batteries or other means of storing

◢ Supercomputer to the Rescue

The engineers at Vestas are planning new wind farms with the help of an IBM supercomputer. The computer analyzes huge amounts of data, including weather reports, satellite images, and sensor information. It then figures out how much energy a wind farm could produce in a particular location. In addition, the system plans where to put each individual turbine so they do not interfere with each other. If one turbine is placed directly behind another, for example, the one in front will take almost all of the energy out of the wind, and the one behind will produce much less energy. The planning process used to take weeks to complete, but IBM's supercomputer can generate results in less than an hour.

power could also help deal with the intermittency of wind power.

Advanced computer processing is also helping engineers at Vestas plan the location and layout of new wind farms. This planning is very important because giant industrial turbines can cost millions of dollars each. Engineers need to make sure the wind farm will produce enough electricity to make up for this cost before they start building.

The construction of new wind farms—on land, out at sea, and in the sky—is likely to rapidly expand. The low cost and excellent efficiency of this renewable energy source make it a popular option.

Maintaining and repairing today's gigantic wind turbines is not a job for those afraid of heights.

SIX

WATER, WAVES, AND HEAT

In addition to sunlight and wind, our planet offers several other sources of renewable energy, including water and geothermal heat. If you have ever been to a natural hot spring, you have experienced geothermal energy. The inside of Earth is extremely hot, and in some places, such as the country of Iceland, this heat rises to the surface, where people can use it to cook food, warm buildings, or generate electricity. Scientists can also drill wells as deep as one mile (1.6 km) to tap into geothermal heat in places where this energy source does not come up to the surface naturally.

Water energy, known as hydropower, is the most common renewable energy in use today. In Norway, it supplies 96.6 percent of the electricity.[1] In dozens of other countries, including Canada and Switzerland, more than 50 percent of the electricity comes from hydropower sources.[2]

Geothermal plants produce more than a quarter of Iceland's electricity.

◢ Is Hydropower Green?

When power plants burn coal, you can see pollution rising into the air in columns of smoke. That smoke contains the gas carbon dioxide. However, hydroelectric power comes from water spinning a turbine. This process certainly seems clean, and it does not produce any smoke. However, when people dam a river to create a reservoir to feed into a hydroelectric plant, that reservoir releases methane gas into the atmosphere. Along with carbon dioxide, methane contributes to the greenhouse effect, which has led to climate change. A reservoir releases the most gas in the years immediately after it is built. The construction kills a lot of plants, and as those plants decay, they release methane. Constructing dams can also disturb local fish, birds, and other wildlife.

Engineers have built water turbines on barges or bridge pylons to generate power without the need for a dam. This dam-free technology could help increase the amount of available hydropower and avoid the problems associated with creating new reservoirs.

People have been using the force of flowing water for centuries. Large waterwheels placed in rivers powered early mills. The flowing current spun the wheel, which powered machinery inside the mill. That same force can be used to turn a generator and produce electricity. Hydropower is more efficient than both solar and wind energy; a hydroelectric plant can convert up to 90 percent of the energy of flowing water into electricity.[3] This power source is relatively inexpensive, too.

Today's hydroelectric power plants typically rely on a dam built across a river. The dam holds water in a reservoir. To produce power, engineers open gates in the dam. Water flows from a height through a gate and down past a turbine that powers a generator. The gravitational energy of the water is converted into electric energy. Unlike intermittent wind and solar power, hydropower is always available as long as there is water in the reservoir. Plus, it is easy to control the amount of power a hydroelectric plant produces by

holding back or releasing water. This technology has not changed much in recent years because it is already so efficient.

However, hydropower is only an option in places with powerful rivers. Some researchers are looking to the ocean as an additional source of water energy. In the United States, more than 50 percent of the population lives within 50 miles (80 km) of the coast.[4] Waves, tides, and even heat trapped in seawater can all provide clean, renewable energy. But these power sources are difficult to capture.

How to Catch a Wave

Wave energy technology is still in the early stages of development. "We may not have even invented the best device yet," said Robert Thresher of the National Renewable Energy Laboratory.[5] Some of the devices that already exist include buoy-like generators that bob on the surface; long, floating structures called attenuators; and machines that sit on shore where the waves crash.

The company Ocean Power Technology has tested its PowerBuoy technology off the coast of New Jersey. The device looks a bit like an orange traffic cone sitting on top of the water. It is connected to a long shaft that hangs below the surface. As the waves go by, the part above the surface bobs up and down. This motion runs a generator. Cables carry the power along the ocean floor and back to shore.

The world's first commercial wave farm, which operated off the coast of Portugal for a short time in 2008, used technology called attenuators. These long, snakelike devices were each composed of several tube-shaped sections that floated on top of the water. Joints between each section moved back and forth as waves went by, powering a generator. This technology also used cables on the ocean floor

The Portuguese wave farm used enormous tubes that floated on the water's surface.

to get the collected electricity back to land. Technical difficulties, including leaks in the tanks that were supposed to be keeping the attenuators floating, caused the project to close after only a few months.

Although wave energy is still years or even decades away from widespread use, it is an exciting field for research and development.

Natural Heat

Swimming at the beach in the tropics is a lot of fun partly because the water is so warm. Earth's oceans absorb a huge amount of sunlight, but only the top layer of the water warms up. Deeper water stays cold. Cutting-edge technology called ocean thermal energy conversion (OTEC) uses this temperature difference to drive turbines that generate electricity.

Meanwhile, in Iceland, a different source of heat provides renewable, clean energy. The natural geography of this country offers easy access to geothermal heat, which provides 25 percent of the country's electricity and heats nine out of ten homes during the winter.[7]

Earth is extremely hot everywhere if you dig down far enough. Magma, composed of molten rocks, makes up most of Earth's mantle, which is the layer directly below the crust. In Iceland and other countries, including Japan and parts of the United States, magma squeezes up close to the surface, where it may erupt from volcanoes as lava. It may also simply heat up groundwater. Steam from these naturally hot pools can turn turbines to generate electricity.

California is home to the largest geothermal energy network in the world, the Geysers. The area contains natural reservoirs of steam, which feed into 14 power plants that provide enough combined power for a city the size of San Francisco.[8]

Researchers are working on new technology to help make this renewable, clean energy source available everywhere, even in places without natural volcanic activity. The most common solution is to drill down to reach deep reservoirs of hot underground water. However, knowing where to drill can be tricky. New mapping techniques can help engineers find natural reserves of hot underground water. Engineers can also create their own reservoirs by pumping water into hot rock formations deep underground. This technology is referred to as hot dry rock geothermal. The process is similar to the disposal of fracking wastewater. Both processes run the risk of causing earthquakes.

◄ Ocean Heat

There are several ways to use ocean heat to generate electricity. The process is known as ocean thermal energy conversion (OTEC). The most common method uses a liquid with a low boiling point, such as ammonia. A large structure pumps in warm seawater to boil the ammonia, and the ammonia vapor turns a turbine to power a generator. Then another pipe brings in cold seawater to turn the ammonia vapor back into a liquid so it can cycle through the process all over again. The company Makai Ocean Engineering is testing this process in Hawaii. It expects the power plant will use up most of the energy it produces only to keep running, but they hope to find ways to improve the technology.

The Makai OTEC plant is on land, but another group is building a similar plant off the shore of the Caribbean island of Martinique. Project leader Emmanuel Brochard said OTEC technology is no longer only a research project: "It is a real, new source of renewable energy."[9]

People have been using geothermal energy from the area of the Geysers since the 1960s.

The Best Renewable Energy

The sun, wind, water, and earth can all provide renewable energy with much less of a negative effect on the environment when compared with fossil fuels. Which is the best choice? It depends on where the power plant will be located.

For example, the Geysers system of power plants takes advantage of one of a few places on Earth where natural steam occurs. In a sunny desert, solar may be a great choice, whereas wind is likely the best option out on an open prairie. Water is the cheapest and most efficient type of renewable energy near a river. And for people living near the ocean, energy from waves, tides, ocean heat, or winds could provide power in the coming decades, though these technologies are still being developed. In the future, the best solution to replace fossil fuels will likely be a combination of all of these renewable resources.

◄ Heat Pumps

Geothermal energy can heat and cool a house without the need for heating oil or natural gas. A ground-source heat pump system only needs a small amount of electricity to run. It supplies three to five times more energy than it takes to power the machinery.

The system relies on the fact that the temperature underground stays almost the same through cold winters and hot summers. On cold days, a pipe carries warm water from the ground up into the house. On hot days, another pipe carries heat from the air down into the ground and stores it there.

Approximately 60,000 new ground-source heat pump systems are installed in the United States each year.[10] That is great progress for renewable energy, but many more homes and buildings install systems that rely on fossil fuels each year.

SEVEN

A BETTER
BATTERY

Many forms of renewable energy face the same challenge: they are not always available. The sun goes down at night and the wind does not always blow. However, people need electricity all the time. The electric grid must constantly balance the supply of electricity coming out of a power generator with the demand.

To make the most of resources such as solar or wind power, people need either a back-up power generator or a good way to save electricity for later. Storing electricity in batteries has typically been more expensive than buying freshly generated power, but batteries are becoming cheaper and more efficient. Large, powerful batteries could soon become part of the electric grid. At the same time, researchers are working to make batteries for handheld devices smaller and longer lasting.

In the future, many homes that generate their own power using the wind or sun may have household batteries that store that power for later use.

Battery Factory

Nevada will soon be home to a 10 million square foot (930,000 sq m) battery factory nicknamed the Gigafactory.[2] Tesla started constructing this manufacturing plant in 2015, and if everything goes according to schedule, the factory will double the number of lithium-ion batteries produced in the world by 2020.[3] Increasing production should help lower the cost of these batteries, which power Tesla's electric cars. Tesla is also going to sell a battery pack called Powerwall directly to homeowners. The company will sell the batteries under the brand Tesla Energy.

Storing Sunlight

Tesla's EVs are already famous. Now, the company is building a factory that will produce a larger version of the car's battery pack for home use. Elon Musk, Tesla's CEO, is also chairman of SolarCity, a company that installs solar panels. This company plans to start offering a home battery along with its solar panel installations.

Tesla and SolarCity are not the first companies to offer storage options for solar. In Germany, engineer Wolfram Walter won an award for innovative renewable product of the year for the invention of a device he calls *Sonnenspeicher*, or "Sun Storage." Walter said he didn't like any of the storage systems that he found for sale: "So I decided, no problem, I will do it better, for me."[1] Walter developed a system of electronics and software that manages the way electricity flows between his solar panels, a battery, and the grid. The invention saves money by using energy more efficiently.

Big and Small

Lithium-ion batteries remain the best rechargeable battery technology available today for electric cars and small devices. The rechargeable batteries work thanks to a chemical reaction that sends lithium atoms from the negative pole of the battery to the positive pole. As they move, they shed

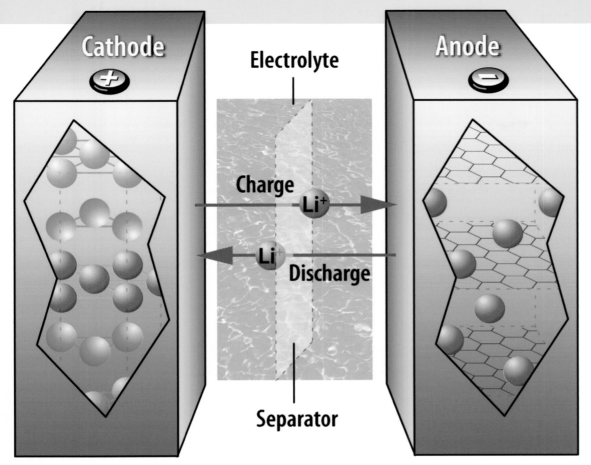

Cathode ⊕

Electrolyte

Anode ⊖

Charge Li^+ →

← Li^+ **Discharge**

Separator

An ion is an atom with a different number of electrons than protons. This difference gives the atom a negative or positive charge. In a lithium-ion battery, atoms of the element lithium travel between the battery's cathode, where electricity flows out of the battery, and anode, where electricity flows in. When the battery is being used to power something, lithium atoms move from the anode to the cathode. When the battery is being recharged, positively charged lithium ions (Li+) move in the reverse direction. A substance called a separator divides the cathode from the anode. A liquid called an electrolyte helps transport the lithium ions through the battery.

electrons, which get put to work as electricity. Charging the battery reverses the direction of the electron movement.

However, lithium-ion batteries have several drawbacks. With time, the battery cannot store as much energy. It also uses toxic chemicals and can burst into flames if not handled correctly. Large

◢ Liquid Metal Batteries

Donald Sadoway of MIT set out to produce a large battery that would be cheaper than current technologies. "If you want to make something dirt cheap, make it out of dirt," said Sadoway.[5] The metals he selected for the battery, magnesium and antimony, can be found in dirt and rocks underground. The battery runs at a scalding 930 degrees Fahrenheit (500°C).[6] At this temperature, the metals melt and stay in liquid form. Liquid metals can last longer and handle higher levels of electric current than solid metals. As the team started building and testing larger and larger batteries, it gave them nicknames. The batteries went from "the hockey puck" to "the pizza." Now, battery company Ambri is selling massive batteries containing hundreds of large cells.

lithium-ion batteries are more dangerous than small ones.

When people need large batteries now, they typically use lead-acid technology. This is the type of battery that helps start the engine in a gas-powered car. Researchers at many universities and companies are racing to produce a large battery that will be safer, cheaper, or more powerful than either lithium-ion or lead-acid technology.

One innovative new battery contains liquid metals. Donald Sadoway, the MIT researcher who invented liquid metal batteries, founded the company Ambri to sell the new technology. Another company, Aquion, uses sodium from salt water inside its battery. Meanwhile, at Lawrence Berkeley National Laboratory, scientists are working to make safer lithium-ion batteries. They are using chemicals that will evaporate instead of burning. The downside is these batteries charge up more slowly than normal lithium-ion batteries, but the team is working to fix this problem.

Meanwhile, as large-scale battery technology improves, tiny batteries for electronics are also getting a makeover. The company SolidEnergy has developed a new lithium-ion battery that is one-half of the size of the one in a typical iPhone but stores twice as much energy.[4] Sakti3 is another company

Breakthrough or Bust?

Battery breakthroughs are exciting, but many times a researcher's big idea never makes it into an actual car or electronic device. The company A123 Systems developed a new, advanced type of lithium-ion battery. But it ran into trouble trying to bring them to the market. It spent more than $300 million on equipment to make the batteries, but one of its major customers cut its orders dramatically, forcing the company to lay off workers.[7]

Envia is another battery company that promised a cheap lithium-ion battery that could store twice as much energy as existing ones. The company planned to produce its product for electric cars. However, this breakthrough was too good to be true. With time, the battery became unreliable.

The chemistry inside a battery is very complex, and even experienced engineers often have trouble understanding why a new battery technology behaves a certain way. It may be a long time before anyone comes up with a new battery technology that can actually replace the ones currently in use.

that says it has improved lithium-ion technology. It uses the same processes that produce thin-film solar cells. However, these companies still have to prove they can scale up and mass produce a product. It is much easier to build a few batteries as prototypes in a laboratory than it is to manufacture millions of them at a reasonable cost for use in real-world devices.

Beyond Batteries

All batteries, big or small, use chemical reactions to store energy. However, there are many other ways to store energy. Pumped water storage is one common method. When a power source is producing more electricity than the grid needs, the system pumps water up a slope and into a pool. When the grid needs electricity, the pool lets the water flow back down, sending it through a hydroelectric turbine.

Coiled magnets can also hold energy. A magnetic field can release its stored energy much more quickly than any other methods. Electricity from solar panels, wind farms, or other sources could also feed into a system that produces hydrogen fuel from water. Then, a fuel cell could act as a battery. Whenever the grid needs electricity, the fuel cell system would take in hydrogen and produce power.

Pumped water storage systems help balance the load on a power grid throughout the day.

Whether we rely on batteries, magnets, pumped water, or other techniques, energy storage is an important complement to any energy production method. Sam Jaffe, founder of the battery company Cygnus Energy Storage, predicts better energy storage will help improve the way we use electricity. He said, "In ten years the grid will be cleaner, less expensive to maintain, and more reliable. And that will be thanks to energy storage technology."[8]

EIGHT

FROM FISSION
TO FUSION

Almost every energy technology that exists relies on sunlight in some form or another. Solar power uses sunlight directly, whereas biofuels and fossil fuels come from plants and animals that grew thanks to sunlight. The sun warms the air and oceans, making wind and ocean thermal power possible. What if we could skip these intermediate steps and create new, miniature suns here on Earth? This is exactly what fusion scientists want to do.

Fusion is the type of nuclear reaction that makes the sun and other stars shine. The extremely strong gravity inside a star pushes atoms close together, causing them to join, or fuse, into new elements. This reaction gives off energy. Scientists have successfully created fusion reactions on Earth, but initiating this reaction requires more energy than can be harnessed from the process. Another type of nuclear reaction, fission, is easier to control. It already provides huge amounts of energy.

Fission is the opposite of fusion. Instead of joining atoms

Fusion energy researchers are attempting to harness the same reaction that powers the sun.

Fission power plants have been in widespread use for more than 50 years.

together, fission breaks them apart. This is the type of reaction happening inside nuclear power plants.

Both fission and fusion produce huge amounts of energy without requiring much fuel. In fact, 2.2 pounds (1 kg) of the most common fuel used in nuclear fission, a form of uranium, contains 2.7 million times the energy of the same amount of coal.[1] However, many people oppose nuclear power due to safety concerns. They are worried about radioactive waste. Nuclear power plants also produce high levels of radiation. During normal operation, shielding protects people from this energy. But if the plant is damaged, the radiation can pose a serious danger.

The Birth of Nuclear Power

In a squash court at the University of Chicago in 1942, Enrico Fermi and his colleagues carefully and secretly constructed a stack of bricks and rods. They named it Chicago Pile-1 (CP1). The team made history when it achieved the world's first controlled nuclear chain reaction. The element uranium provided the fuel for the reaction.

◢ The Manhattan Project

The US government sponsored Enrico Fermi's experimental nuclear reactor as part of the secret Manhattan Project during World War II (1939–1945). Countries on both sides of the war knew it was possible to use nuclear fission to create incredibly powerful weapons, so they raced to master the technology before their enemies. After Fermi's success in Chicago, he joined a group of scientists led by Robert Oppenheimer at Los Alamos National Laboratory in New Mexico. By 1945, the team had built and tested nuclear bombs. The United States made the controversial decision to drop them on the cities of Hiroshima and Nagasaki in Japan, resulting in hundreds of thousands of deaths from the explosions of the bombs and from the long-term effects of radiation poisoning.

Uranium occurs naturally as a heavy metal inside rocks. When uranium gets hit with a neutron, one of the types of particles that makes up atoms, it breaks apart. This fission reaction gives off energy and more neutrons. These free neutrons can then crash into other uranium atoms, causing a cascade of fission reactions that keeps giving off energy until either the neutrons or the uranium run out. The element plutonium is similar to uranium, and it can also set off a chain reaction.

In a nuclear bomb, the reaction runs out of control, producing a massive and deadly explosion. However, in CP1 or in a modern nuclear power plant, the reaction keeps a steady pace. Power plants use control rods made of a material that absorbs neutrons. Adding control rods slows down or stops the reaction, whereas removing them speeds it up. Also, the fuel for a reactor contains relatively little enriched fuel, which is a special form of uranium or plutonium that divides very easily. A bomb must contain almost entirely enriched fuel. A nuclear power plant cannot explode like a bomb.

The destruction of the Fukushima Daiichi reactors prompted renewed worries about the safety of nuclear power.

Safe or Deadly?

In May 2015, a total of 437 nuclear power plants around the world provided more than 11 percent of the planet's electricity.[2] In France, nuclear power provides 75 percent of the electricity.[3] The country sells extra electricity from its nuclear plants to other nations. This energy source does not pollute the air or produce greenhouse gases. Statistically speaking, nuclear power plants are very safe; they cause fewer deaths than most other types of energy technology in use today. More people have died making solar panels than have died working in or around nuclear plants.

However, in a disaster, a nuclear plant could potentially cause widespread harm. An earthquake in Japan in 2011 caused the Fukushima Daiichi nuclear power plant to melt down, putting many people in

History's most notorious nuclear disaster, the explosion of the Chernobyl plant in Ukraine, forced the abandonment of nearby cities.

danger. Approximately 100,000 people had to leave their homes.[4] Both the fuel and waste from nuclear power plants are radioactive. Radioactive materials decay, or lose particles, over time. These particles radiate away from the material. At low levels, radioactivity is a normal part of the natural world and is not dangerous. If a person gets exposed to too much of it, though, he or she can get sick or even die. For these reasons, many people are against nuclear power.

However, nuclear technology continues improving, and there may be no good reason to be afraid of it. Today's nuclear power plants contain advanced safety systems that help prevent accidents and contain radioactive materials. Some plants will shut themselves down in an emergency. Researchers have also developed methods to recycle nuclear waste so it can be reused in current reactors, or in new, cutting-edge reactor designs. One such reactor, the fast neutron reactor, or breeder reactor, is an old idea that is gaining popularity today as engineers improve its design. It uses fuel even more efficiently than other reactor types.

◄ The Waste Debate

Yucca Mountain rises from the desert about an hour's drive northwest of Las Vegas, Nevada. The United States government selected this site in 1987 as the best place to store nuclear waste. In 2002, President George W. Bush approved the site, but the mountain still does not house any waste because so many people are fighting against the decision. They worry the waste could contaminate the area. In the meantime, most nuclear plants store their waste on-site, either in pools of water or in special steel containers. Nuclear energy is so efficient that it does not produce very much waste at all. If you were to stack all of the waste ever produced from all of the nuclear power plants in the world, it would fit in a football field at a depth of approximately eight yards (7.3 m).[5] If new reactor technologies take off, much of this waste could be reused as fuel.

A Sun in a Bottle

Despite advances in nuclear fission technology, the fuel poses potential problems. Earth contains limited amounts of uranium and plutonium, and many people would feel safer relying on less radioactive materials for energy. Nuclear fusion, on the other hand, can run on fuel made from the hydrogen found in seawater. Fusion could produce much more energy than fission.

Scientists can create fusion reactions, but they cannot sustain them or control them enough to produce power. The process to get the reaction started uses high-tech, costly machinery and consumes more energy than the reaction produces. "Fusion is an expensive science, because you're trying to build a sun in a bottle," said Michael Williams of Princeton University.[6]

Fusion in the sun, the star at the center of our solar system, keeps going thanks to the sun's immense gravity. Most fusion reactors, on the other hand, convert hydrogen into a very energetic form called plasma. This heated state of matter is found within stars. It can also be seen on Earth in neon signs. Reactors use intense heat and pressure to force atoms to join together. Plasma is difficult to control. It would destroy any ordinary container. Most fusion reactor designs use the power of magnets to hold the plasma.

One promising fusion reactor design is called a tokamak. This powerful machine is usually shaped like a doughnut. Magnets wrap around the outside of the tube, and the plasma flows through the inside. Some scientists believe a more spherical shape would be better at containing plasma.

Scientists at Lawrence Livermore National Laboratory in California are using groups of lasers instead of magnets to achieve fusion. In 2013, they conducted an experiment in which they aimed 192

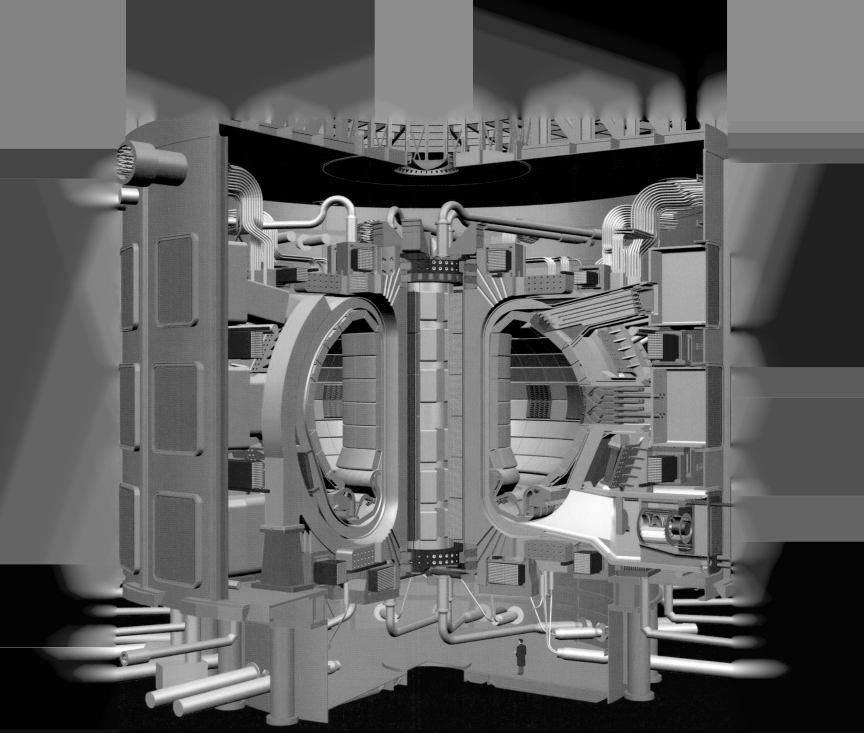

◢ A Mighty Doughnut

Several experimental tokamak fusion reactors already exist. With this technology, bigger is usually better because a larger reactor does a better job at controlling plasma. An international group of scientists is building the biggest tokamak yet in France. It is called ITER, which comes from a Latin word meaning "the way." When ITER is complete, the $18 billion doughnut-shaped machine will weigh as much as three Eiffel towers.[8] The project's goal is to produce ten times more power than it takes to run the reactor.[9]

lasers at a pellet of hydrogen to produce a fusion reaction. The reaction created slightly more energy than it used up, but it did not sustain itself, lasting only for a fraction of a second. "This is closer than anyone's gotten before," said Omar Hurricane, one of the researchers.[7]

A test tokamak machine in Italy has been in operation since the 1990s.

NINE

THE FUTURE OF ENERGY

Energy is all around us in the form of sunlight, waves, wind, and water. It is beneath our feet in pools of oil and gas and geothermal heat, and it is locked up inside animal and plant waste and even inside atoms of uranium and plutonium. A range of technologies captures energy from all of these forms and converts it into fuel or electricity humans can use.

In the near future, people will seek to find better ways to harvest energy from renewable, clean sources such as sunlight, wind, water, and nuclear fusion to protect the environment from further damage from fossil fuels. Experts also want to improve the ways that people transfer, store, and use energy. If these processes can be made more efficient, less energy will need to be generated in the first place.

The future of energy will involve not just new generation technologies, but also new and more efficient ways to transmit that power.

The Smart Grid

Creating a smarter grid will require installing new equipment throughout the country.

One big idea that could transform our energy future is the smart grid. Right now, the US electric grid is an incredibly complex network of approximately 9,200 power generators, including power plants and wind and solar farms that feed into 300,000 miles (480,000 km) of power lines.[1] Each year, more than one-half of the energy that enters this system gets lost along the way. It escapes from power plants or power lines, usually as heat.

Today, human operators have to constantly watch the grid to make sure the amount of electricity power plants produce can satisfy the demand from energy consumers. The power typically flows only in one direction: from the plant and into homes and businesses. Some power plants called peaker plants sit around doing nothing for most of the year. They are there to help supply electricity on days when demand is very high, such as on very hot days when many people turn on their air conditioners.

A smart grid would balance electricity supply and demand on its own. To do this, electricity and information would flow in all directions. Every part of the system would send information to the other parts to use energy more efficiently. For example, a person's dishwasher, television, and other appliances would tell the grid how much electricity they need, and solar panels, wind turbines, and power plants would communicate back with how much electricity is available. Then, some of the appliances would adjust to use more or less electricity. For example, a dishwasher might shut off its heater or delay its wash cycle for a short time. Solar panels on rooftops or home battery systems could add electricity into the system. The smart grid would rely on advanced computer programs with artificial intelligence to make sure the electricity goes where and when it is needed most. Smart grid systems are now under development.

Wireless World

In 2015, a company introduced small personal solar panels that attach to backpack straps.

The grid, smart or not, requires thousands of miles of wire to transfer power. People do not need wires to send text messages or play videos over an Internet connection. Why do you still have to plug a cell phone into the wall to charge the battery? One problem with transferring electricity wirelessly is making sure the signal is strong enough to power a device but will not damage living things. Researchers are working on solutions to this problem.

One day, devices may either continually charge themselves from an invisible grid or generate their own power with tiny solar panels or power generation devices. Robots, music players, television screens, and other devices that have not been invented yet could all work continuously without power cords.

The technology to make this future possible is under development, and some companies have already released wireless power products. Most wireless charging technologies use a charging station or pad instead of a plug. They rely on induction. In this process, a metal coil inside the charging pad produces a magnetic field. A similar coil inside the device picks up this field and gets electricity from it. However, the user still has to plug in the charging pad, and the device and charging pad must be touching and be precisely lined up.

New technologies are increasing the distance at which wireless power will work. In 2007, a team at MIT lit up a light bulb at a distance of seven feet (2.1 m) from its power source.[2] They went on to start a company called WiTricity. WiTricity envisions a future in which homes and businesses set up WiTricity stations so people can charge batteries on the go.

WIRELESS
CHARGING

The company WiTricity began when MIT professor Marin Soljačić's beeping cell phone woke him up in the middle of the night. It was alerting him to its almost-dead battery. "It occurred to me that it would be so great if the thing took care of its own charging," he said.[3] His team at MIT used a technique called magnetic resonance to develop a new kind of wireless charging technology.

When two objects are resonant, it means they are vibrating or moving at the same rate. These objects can exchange energy very easily. For example, an opera singer who reaches a certain pitch and holds it can break a glass. This happens because the glass starts to vibrate at that precise pitch, and it vibrates more energetically the louder her voice gets. The glass and the musical note are resonant.

To transfer electricity with this method, one copper coil produces a vibrating magnetic field. Another copper coil in a nearby device picks up the field and vibrates at the same rate. The field can then provide electricity to the device.

WiTricity is working with auto manufacturer Toyota on a new EV that will not need to plug in. It is also collaborating with a health-care company on a plan to wirelessly charge medical equipment.

A WiTricity car and charging panel were shown off at the 2015 International Consumer Electronics Show in Las Vegas, Nevada.

Solar roadways and bike paths feature a thick layer of glass to prevent damage and a rough surface for traction.

Wireless charging has other exciting applications. Imagine a future in which electric cars and buses charge themselves as they drive thanks to chargers built into the road itself. A bus system that runs on this type of electric road already exists in South Korea, and one is being built in Sweden.

Beyond the Grid

Electric roads could draw power from cables connected to the grid or directly from the sun. Advances in solar energy and nanotechnology could allow every surface we own to become its own power generator. "The power plant of tomorrow is no power plant," said Justin Hall-Tipping, who manages the nanotechnology company NanoHoldings. "The grid of tomorrow is no grid, and energy, clean efficient energy, will one day be free."[4]

This may sound far-fetched, but it already happens every day in the woods. The leaves on plants capture sunlight and turn it into energy using a process called photosynthesis. In this process, the leaf breaks apart water into oxygen and hydrogen. The oxygen gets released into the air, and the plant uses the hydrogen to make its own food.

◂Leaf Power

Daniel Nocera of Harvard University has created an artificial leaf that produces hydrogen fuel from sunlight and water. The device is the size of a credit card. You place it into water, then bathe it in sunlight, and it breaks apart the water molecules into pure hydrogen and oxygen. Researchers at MIT have also reproduced photosynthesis, but they did it using a virus. The virus cannot make anyone sick. The team designed it to split water.

One of the major challenges now is to change the way people use energy. If we start using hydrogen fuel cells in our homes and cars, Nocera's leaf and the MIT team's virus could provide a clean, renewable source of fuel. "And this is my ultimate vision and I believe it will happen sometime," said Nocera. "Your house will be its own gas station."[5]

Space Mining

Many asteroids and planets in outer space contain water, gases, precious metals, and other useful materials. In the future, space expeditions may extract these resources to produce fuels or to return them to Earth. NASA is launching the spacecraft OSIRIS-REx in 2016 to bring back material from an asteroid. The mission will help scientists learn how we would go about exploring and mining asteroids for the resources they contain.

We do not have to fly all the way to asteroids to go space mining. Our moon is full of frozen water that could be processed to make hydrogen and oxygen. These are the main ingredients in rocket fuel. Being able to refuel rockets on the moon could make it easier to reach other destinations in space. The moon also has something that is very rare on Earth: helium-3, a form of the gas that fills birthday balloons. This particular type of helium has a structure that makes it a perfect choice as a fuel in a nuclear fusion reactor.

Scientists and engineers are working on a range of ideas that would allow the things we own to produce their own energy. Artificial leaves mimic the process of photosynthesis to produce hydrogen from water. This hydrogen could feed a fuel cell to power a car or device. At the same time, advances in nanotechnology could allow us to build miniature power plants or tiny batteries that could constantly harvest and store energy, then provide on-demand electricity.

Into the Future

Some people are looking to space for new energy sources. Space exploration could open up new worlds full of potential fuel. It may be possible to harvest fuel sources from planets, moons, or asteroids in the far reaches of outer space. Space mining could produce fuels to power spacecraft or space stations.

Energy is what drives human civilization forward. Liquid fuels have allowed us to travel quickly in cars, airplanes, and even rockets. Electricity and batteries have allowed us to connect with each other through cell phone networks and the Internet. Renewable power sources use sunlight, waves, and Earth's underground heat to provide clean electricity. Researchers are working to make all of these technologies safer, cheaper, and more efficient. The future of energy technology is wide open.

◂ Nanogenerator

Michael Strano and his team at MIT discovered a new way to generate electricity using a tiny piece of yarn and some fuel. The yarn is made of special carbon atoms, known as carbon nanotubes, coiled together and coated in fuel. Adding a pulse of heat to one side of the yarn creates a wave of heat. They call their discovery a thermopower wave. "It can push electrons out of this tube like squeezing toothpaste out of a tube," explained Strano.[6] The reaction converts a burning fuel, such as ethanol, into electricity, but the heat does not destroy the nanotubes. They can be used over and over again. For its size, this nanogenerator produces as much as 14 times more power than a lithium-ion battery.[7]

ESSENTIAL FACTS

Key Discoveries

» **Hydraulic Fracturing:** Also known as fracking, this is a mining technique that cracks apart rocks deep below the earth. Then, engineers can drill out trapped natural gas or oil. This breakthrough led to a natural gas boom in the United States.

» **Hydrogen Fuel Cell:** This technology is similar to a battery and could power electric cars or even our homes and businesses. A fuel cell combines hydrogen gas with oxygen from the air to make electricity. This chemical reaction gives off water and heat, so it does not pollute the air.

» **Nuclear Energy:** When atoms break apart in a nuclear fission reaction or join together during a nuclear fusion reaction, a huge amount of energy is released. Fission makes nuclear weapons and nuclear power plants possible. Scientists are still working to build a device that can control and sustain a fusion reaction.

» **Solar Cells:** This technology converts sunlight into electricity. Thin or transparent solar cells could cover windows and other surfaces to provide energy whenever the sun is shining.

Key Players

» **France:** Nuclear power plants generate most of France's energy. This country is also home to ITER, a gigantic fusion reactor that is under construction.

» **Massachusetts Institute of Technology (MIT):** Researchers at MIT have made numerous breakthroughs in energy technology, including transparent solar cells, liquid metal batteries, wireless electricity, and a nanogenerator.

» **Tesla Motors:** This company produces electric cars and develops improved battery technology.

» **The US Department of Energy:** This government branch provides money and support to numerous clean energy companies and research projects. Steven Chu served as the Secretary of Energy through 2013.

Key Tools and Technologies

» **Batteries:** Batteries use chemical reactions to store energy. Lithium-ion batteries are the best rechargeable battery technology available today for electric cars and small devices.

» **Biofuels:** Plant matter or animal fats can be processed to produce fuel that can be burned in combustion engines. These fuels produce fewer harmful fumes than fossil fuels.

» **Electric Vehicle:** A plug-in electric vehicle (EV) runs on batteries that need to be recharged. A hybrid EV uses a battery and liquid fuel.

» **Turbines:** A turbine has blades that spin around, just like the propeller on an airplane. In a wind turbine, air turns the blades, and in a hydropower dam or tidal power system, water makes them spin. To produce power, a generator attached to the turbine converts the spinning motion into electricity.

Future Outlook

In the future, people will need to find better ways to harvest energy from renewable, clean sources such as sunlight, wind, water, and nuclear fusion before fossil fuels cause too much harm to the environment. New technologies will also improve the ways that we transfer, store, and use energy.

Quote

"The power plant of tomorrow is no power plant. . . . The grid of tomorrow is no grid, and energy, clean efficient energy, will one day be free."

—*Justin Hall–Tipping*

GLOSSARY

aerodynamics

The study of how air moves around objects.

biofuel

Fuel made from plant matter, animal fats, or other organic waste.

biomass

Plant matter and animal parts that can be processed to produce fuels.

carbon capture and storage (CCS)

A process that separates carbon dioxide from other gases and then puts the carbon dioxide in a place where it cannot escape into the air.

carbon dioxide

A gas that is released when people breathe and when fossil fuels are burned.

climate change

A process affecting the planet that is causing temperatures around the world to rise.

diesel

An alternative liquid fossil fuel sometimes used instead of gasoline.

emission

Gas and other waste that vehicles and power plants let out into the air when they run.

ethanol

An alcohol-based fuel made from plants such as sugarcane, corn, or algae.

greenhouse gas

A substance, such as carbon dioxide, that causes the planet to heat up when too much of it builds up in the atmosphere.

heliostat

A device that focuses sunlight on a specific area using a mirror.

hydraulic fracturing (fracking)

A technique that uses water to break apart shale rocks to extract trapped reserves of natural gas.

intermittency

Stopping and starting over time instead of remaining constant.

internal combustion engine

An engine that burns a fuel in order to drive pistons that provide the force needed to move a vehicle forward.

lead-acid battery

A rechargeable battery commonly found in gas-powered car engines.

liquid metal battery

A new battery technology that operates at a high temperature.

lithium-ion battery

An advanced rechargeable battery found in computers, cell phones, and some electric vehicles.

nanotechnology

The assembly and manipulation of structures at the level of atoms or molecules to carry out agricultural functions.

petroleum

Also known as crude oil, this fossil fuel can be processed into heating oil or gasoline.

photoelectric effect

A property of some materials that allows them to convert sunlight into electricity.

pitch

Movement around a horizontal axis.

yaw

Movement around a vertical axis.

ADDITIONAL RESOURCES

Selected Bibliography

Musk, Elon. "The Mind Behind Tesla, SpaceX, SolarCity." *TED*. TED, Feb. 2013. Web. 23 July 2015.

Pump. Dir. Joshua Tickell and Rebecca Harrell Tickell, 2014. Film.

Further Readings

Carmichael, L. E. *Hybrid and Electric Vehicles*. Minneapolis: Abdo, 2013. Print.

Challoner, Jack. *Energy*. New York: DK, 2012. Print.

Higgins, Melissa. *Wind Energy*. Minneapolis: Abdo, 2013. Print.

Zuchora-Walske, Christine. *Solar Energy*. Minneapolis: Abdo, 2013. Print.

Websites

To learn more about Cutting-Edge Science and Technology, visit **booklinks.abdopublishing.com**. These links are routinely monitored and updated to provide the most current information available.

For More Information

For more information on this subject, contact or visit the following organizations:

The National Energy Education Development Project (NEED)
8408 Kao Circle
Manassas, VA 20110
703-257-1117
http://www.need.org

The NEED Project works with students, teachers, businesses, and governments to create an energy-conscious society.

National Renewable Energy Laboratory (NREL)
15013 Denver West Parkway
Golden, CO 80401
303-275-3000
http://www.nrel.gov

Researchers at NREL look for creative solutions to energy challenges using clean, renewable technologies.

SOURCE NOTES

Chapter 1. Electric Cars

1. David Biello. "Why Electric Cars Will Fail . . . and Have Already Triumphed." *Scientific American*. Scientific American, 20 May 2011. Web. 29 Apr. 2015.

2. "Technology." *Tesla Motors*. Tesla Motors, 2015. Web. 21 Apr. 2015.

3. Elon Musk. "The Mind behind Tesla, SpaceX, SolarCity." *TED*. TED, Feb. 2013. Web. 25 Aug. 2015.

4. "Fossil Fuel Energy Consumption (% of Total)." *World Bank*. World Bank, 2015. Web. 30 Apr. 2015.

5. "Monthly Plug-In Sales Scorecard." *Inside EVs*. Inside EVs, 2015. Web. 1 May 2015.

6. *Pump*. Dir. Joshua Tickell and Rebecca Harrell Tickell. 2014. Film.

7. Elon Musk. "The Mind behind Tesla, SpaceX, SolarCity." *TED*. TED, Feb. 2013. Web. 25 Aug. 2015.

8. Ibid.

9. Ibid.

10. Ibid.

11. Margaret Kane. "eBay Picks Up PayPal for $1.5 Billion." *CNET*. CNET, 8 July 2002. Web. 1 May 2015.

12. "Graphene Supercapacitors Ready for Electric Vehicle Energy Storage, Say Korean Engineers." *MIT Technology Review*. MIT, 12 Nov. 2013. Web. 29 Apr. 2015.

13. "Fuel Cell Electric Vehicles." *US Department of Energy*. US Department of Energy, n.d. Web. 29 Apr. 2015.

14. "What Is US Electricity Generation by Energy Source?" *US Energy Information Administration*. US Energy Information Administration, 31 Mar. 2015. Web. 25 Aug. 2015.

15. Lawrence Ulrich. "G.M.'s Fuel-Cell Test: 100 Cars, No Charge." *New York Times*. New York Times, 9 Dec. 2007. Web. 25 Aug. 2015.

Chapter 2. Fossil Fuels

1. Bjorn Carey. "Q&A: Steven Chu on Returning to Stanford, His Time as U.S. Energy Secretary." *Stanford News*. Stanford, 15 May 2013. Web. 25 Aug. 2015.

2. Steven Chu. "Letter from Secretary Steven Chu to Energy Department Employees." *US Department of Energy*. US Department of Energy, 1 Feb. 2013. Web. 19 May 2015.

3. David Biello. "What Will Steven Chu's Energy Legacy Be?" *Scientific American*. Scientific American, 1 Feb. 2013. Web. 29 Apr. 2015.

4. "Canada Opens a Coal-fired Plant with CCS Technology." *Institute for Energy Research*. Institute for Energy Research, 21 Oct. 2015. Web. 19 May 2015.

5. "Boundary Dam Carbon Capture Project." *SaskPower*. SaskPower, 2014. Web. 19 May 2015.

6. "Reducing America's Energy Dependence." *Natural Resources Defense Council*. Natural Resources Defense Council, 2 July 2004. Web. 22 Apr. 2015.

7. David Stanway. "China Approves Massive New Coal Capacity Despite Pollution Fears." *Reuters*. Reuters, 7 Jan. 2014. Web. 10 May 2015.

8. "What Is US Electricity Generation by Energy Source?" *US Energy Information Administration*. US Energy Information Administration, 31 Mar. 2015. Web. 25 Aug. 2015.

9. "Oil Reserves." *BP*. BP, 2015. Web. 10 May 2015.

10. "Where Is Coal Found?" *World Coal Association*. World Coal Association, n.d. Web. 10 May 2015.

11. Tim Worstall. "Ten Things to Know About Fracking." *Forbes*. Forbes, 21 June 2011. Web. 10 May 2015.

12. Rivka Galchen. "Weather Underground." *New Yorker*. New Yorker, 13 Apr. 2015. Web. 19 May 2015.

13. Gregory Zuckerman and Robert Russ. "Gregory Zuckerman on the Frackers and the Energy Revolution." *EconTalk*. EconTalk, 23 June 2014. Web. 10 May 2015.

14. Mark P. Mills. "Big Data And Microseismic Imaging Will Accelerate The Smart Drilling Oil And Gas Revolution." *Forbes*. Forbes, 8 May 2013. Web. 19 May 2015.

15. Jad Mouawad. "Estimate Places Natural Gas Reserves 35% Higher." *New York Times*. New York Times, 17 June 2009. Web. 10 May 2015.

Chapter 3. Renewable Fuel

1. "How Much Ethanol Is in Gasoline and How Does It Affect Fuel Economy?" *US Energy Information Administration*. US Energy Information Administration, 3 Apr. 2015. Web. 1 June 2015.

2. Michael Hannon, et al. "Biofuels from Algae: Challenges and Potential." *Biofuels* 1.5 (2010): 763–784. Web. 1 June 2015.

3. David Biello. "Can Algae Feed the World and Fuel the Planet? A Q & A with Craig Venter." *Scientific American*. Scientific American, 15 Nov. 2011. Web. 1 June 2015.

4. *Pump*. Dir. Joshua Tickell and Rebecca Harrell Tickell. 2014. Film.

5. Ibid.

6. Nicole Davis. "Turkey Fuel? Factory to Turn Guts Into Crude Oil." *National Geographic*. National Geographic, 25 Nov. 2003. Web. 1 June 2015.

7. "Hydrogen Production: Natural Gas Reforming." *US Department of Energy*. US Department of Energy, 3 Apr. 2015. Web. 1 June 2015.

8. "Discovery in Alternative Energy Production May Be Breakthrough for Hydrogen-Fueled Vehicles." *Virginia Tech News*. Virginia Tech, 7 Apr. 2015. Web. 25 Aug. 2015.

Chapter 4. Solar Power

1. "Solar Energy." *National Geographic*. National Geographic, n.d. Web. 7 May 2015.

2. Elon Musk. "The Mind behind Tesla, SpaceX, SolarCity." *TED*. TED, Feb. 2013. Web. 25 Aug. 2015.

3. Philip Oltermann. "World's First Solar Cycle Lane Opening in the Netherlands." *Guardian*. Guardian, 5 Nov. 2014. Web. 19 May 2015.

4. "SolaRoad Produces More Energy than Expected." *SolaRoad*. SolaRoad, 7 May 2015. Web. 19 May 2015.

5. Tatsuo Saga. "Advances in Crystalline Silicon Solar Cell Technology for Industrial Mass Production." *NPG Asia Materials* (2010): 2, 96–102. Web. 8 May 2015.

6. Meera Senthilingam. "A Brighter Future: Five Ideas That Will Change Solar Energy." *CNN*. CNN, 17 Dec. 2014. Web. 10 May 2015.

7. Mark Schwartz. "Perovskites Provide Big Boost to Silicon Solar Cells, Stanford Study Finds." *Stanford University*. Stanford University, 15 Jan. 2015. Web. 10 May 2015.

8. David Biello. "Solar Power Lightens Up with Thin-Film Technology." *Scientific American*. Scientific American, 25 Apr. 2008. Web. 8 May 2015.

9. Thomas W. Overton "Plant of the Year: Ivanpah Solar Electric Generating System Earns POWER's Highest Honor." *Power Magazine*. Power Magazine, 1 Aug. 2014. Web. 10 May 2015.

10. Mark Strauss. "Take a Look at the World's Largest Solar Thermal Farm." *Smithsonian Magazine*. Smithsonian, Nov. 2012. Web. 10 May 2015.

11. Kate Shaw Yoshida. "Who Needs Sunlight? In Arizona, Solar Power Never Sleeps." *Ars Technica*. Ars Technica, 18 Feb. 2014. Web. 10 May 2015.

12. Nancy W. Stauffer. "Transparent Solar Cells." *MIT Energy Initiative*. MIT, 20 June 2013. Web. 19 May 2015.

13. Ibid.

14. "Made in IBM Labs: Collaboration Aims to Harness the Energy of 2,000 Suns." *IBM*. IBM, 22 Apr. 2013. Web. 26 Aug. 2015.

15. Ibid.

Chapter 5. Wind Energy

1. "Wind Vision." *US Department of Energy*. US Department of Energy, March 2015. Web. 18 May 2015.

2. "What Is US Electricity Generation by Energy Source?" *US Energy Information Administration*. US Energy Information Administration, 31 Mar. 2015. Web. 25 Aug. 2015.

3. "Renewable Energy Fact Sheet: Wind Turbines." *US Environmental Protection Agency*. US Environmental Protection Agency, Aug. 2013. Web. 18 May 2015.

4. "Solar Panel Efficiency." *Pure Energies*. Pure Energies, n.d. Web. 26 Aug. 2015.

5. Christine Blackman. "High-Altitude Winds: The Greatest Source of Concentrated Energy on Earth." *Stanford News*. Stanford, 23 June 2009. Web. 18 May 2015.

6. "The View From the World's Biggest Wind Turbine." *Bloomberg Business*. Bloomberg, 4 Feb. 2015. Web. 18 May 2015.

7. Mike Crawford. "Wind Turbines Get Bigger and Smarter." *ASME*. ASME, July 2013. Web. 18 May 2015.

8. Rob Matheson. "Wind Energy Reaches Greater Heights." *MIT Energy Initiative*. MIT, 6 Nov. 2014. Web. 19 May 2015.

9. Ibid.

10. Kristin Majcher. "Is Offshore Wind Making Any Progress?" *MIT Technology Review*. MIT, 16 Apr. 2015. Web. 19 April 2015.

11. "World's Largest Offshore Wind Farm Opens in the UK." *Department of Energy & Climate Change*. Department of Energy & Climate Change, 4 July 2013. Web. 18 May 2015.

12. Zachary Shahan. "Google Buys Makani Wind Power (Kite Power Company)." *CleanTechnica*. CleanTechnica, 24 May 2013. Web. 19 May 2015.

Chapter 6. Water, Waves, and Heat

1. "Electricity Production from Hydroelectric Sources (% of Total)." *The World Bank*. The World Bank, 2012. Web. 19 May 2015.

2. Anne-Marie Corley. "The Future of Hydropower." *IEEE Spectrum*. IEEE, 1 June 2010. Web. 19 May 2015.

3. "Hydroelectric Power." *Alberta Agricultural and Forestry*. Alberta Agricultural and Forestry, 29 May 2015. Web. 26 Aug. 2015.

4. "Marine and Hydrokinetic Resource Assessment and Characterization." *US Department of Energy*. US Department of Energy, n.d. Web. 19 May 2015.

5. Dave Levitan. "Why Wave Power Has Lagged Far Behind as Energy Source." *Yale Environment 360*. Yale, 28 Apr. 2014. Web. 28 Apr. 2015.

6. Renewable Northwest. "Wave & Tidal Energy Technology." *Renewable Northwest*. Renewable Northwest, 2009. Web. 1 June 2015.

7. "Geothermal." *Orkustofnun National Energy Authority*. Orkustofnun National Energy Authority, n.d. Web. 19 May 2015.

8. "About Geothermal Energy." *The Geysers*. The Geysers, n.d. Web. 19 May 2015.

9. Rachel Courtland. "Ocean Thermal Energy: Back From the Deep." *IEEE Spectrum*. IEEE Spectrum, 29 Aug. 2014. Web. 1 June 2015.

10. "How Geothermal Energy Works." *Union of Concerned Scientists*. Union of Concerned Scientists, 22 Dec. 2014. Web. 1 June 2015.

Chapter 7. A Better Battery

1. Peter Thomson. "How Do You Catch the Sun to Make Electricity at Night? This German Inventor Has an Answer." *PRI*. PRI, 6 Apr. 2015. Web. 19 April 2015.

2. Klint Finley. "Tesla Isn't an Automaker. It's a Battery Company." *Wired*. Wired, 22 Apr. 2015. Web. 1 June 2015.

3. Angus MacKenzie. "Tesla's Gigafactory to Significantly Reduce Li-Ion Battery Production Costs by 2020." *Gizmag*. Gizmag, 27 Feb. 2014. Web. 1 June 2015.

4. Kevin Bullis. "A Battery for Electronics That Lasts Twice as Long." *MIT Technology Review*. MIT, 2 Feb. 2015. Web. 27 May 2015.

5. Donald Sadoway. "The Missing Link to Renewable Energy." *TED*. TED, Mar. 2012. Web. 26 Aug. 2015.

6. Martin LaMonica. "Ambri's Better Battery." *MIT Technology Review*. MIT, 18 Feb. 2013. Web. 1 June 2015.

7. Kevin Bullis. "What Happened to A123?" *MIT Technology Review*. MIT, 25 May 2012. Web. 1 June 2015.

8. Klint Finley. "Tesla Isn't an Automaker. It's a Battery Company." *Wired*. Wired, 22 Apr. 2015. Web. 1 June 2015.

Chapter 8. From Fission to Fusion

1. "Coal Equivalent." *European Nuclear Society*. European Nuclear Society, n.d. Web. 25 May 2015.

2. "Plans For New Reactors Worldwide." *World Nuclear Association*. World Nuclear Association, May 2015. Web. 25 May 2015.

3. "France" *World Nuclear Association*. World Nuclear Association, Oct. 2014. Web. 25 May 2015.

4. "Fukushima Accident." *World Nuclear Association*. World Nuclear Association, Oct. 2014. Web. 25 May 2015.

5. "On-Site Storage of Nuclear Waste." *Nuclear Energy Institute*. Nuclear Energy Institute, 2015. Web. 27 May 2015.

6. Dino Grandoni. "Why It's Taking The US So Long To Make Fusion Energy Work." *Huffington Post*. Huffington Post, 20 Jan. 2015. Web. 26 May 2015.

7. David Biello. "High-Powered Lasers Deliver Fusion Energy Breakthrough." *Scientific American*. Scientific American, 12 Feb. 2014. Web. 26 May 2015.

8. Daniel Clery. "The New Shape of Fusion." *Science*. Science, 22 May 2015. Web. 25 May 2015.

9. "The International ITER Project for Fusion: Why?" *ITER*. ITER, 2015. Web. 1 June 2015.

Chapter 9. The Future of Energy

1. "The Smart Grid." *US Department of Energy*. US Department of Energy, n.d. Web. 1 June 2015.

2. Franklin Hadley. "Goodbye Wires!" *MIT News*. MIT, 7 June 2007. Web. 1 June 2015.

3. Ibid.

4. Justin Hall-Tipping. "Freeing Energy from the Grid." *TED*. TED, July 2011. Web. 26 Aug. 2015.

5. Jack Hitt. "The Artificial Leaf Is Here. Again." *New York Times*. New York Times, 29 Mar. 2014. Web. 1 June 2015.

6. Michael Strano. "Harnessing the Energy of Thermopower Waves: Dr. Michael Strano at TEDxEmbryRiddle." *TEDx*. TEDx, 7 Feb. 2013. Web. 29 May 2015.

7. Ibid.

INDEX

About the Author

Kathryn Hulick lives in Massachusetts with her husband and their new baby, Seth. They like to hike, read, visit the ocean, and play with their dog, Maya. Kathryn also loves working in her garden, where the sun provides energy for vegetables and flowers. She hopes that one day soon, sunlight will power her home and car, too.